The Life of

MARY

and Birth of Jesus

THE ANCIENT
INFANCY GOSPEL OF JAMES

The Life of
MARY
and Birth of Jesus

THE ANCIENT
INFANCY GOSPEL OF JAMES

RONALD F. HOCK

EDITOR
Ray Riegert

ULYSSES PRESS
Berkeley, California

Photo credits: Botticelli "Madonna of the Magnificat" and Giotto "The Birth of the Virgin" and "The Betrothal of the Virgin," Alinari/Art Resource, NY; all other Giotto paintings, Scala/Art Resource, NY; "Joseph's Dream," "The Virgin Receiving the Skein of Wool" and "The Flight into Egypt," Vatican Library; "The Presentation of the Virgin in the Temple," Hirmer Verlag GmbH.

Published by:

Ulysses Press
P.O. Box 3440
Berkeley, CA 94703-3440

Library of Congress Cataloging-in-Publication Data

Hock, Ronald F., 1944–
    The life of Mary and birth of Jesus : the Ancient Infancy Gospel of James / Ronald F. Hock.
        p. cm.
    Includes English translation of the Protevangelium Jacobi (Infancy Gospel of James).
    ISBN 1-56975-079-3 (hardcover)
    1. Protevangelium Jacobi—Criticism, interpretation, etc. 2. Mary, Blessed Virgin, Saint—Biography. 3. Jesus Christ—Nativity. I. Protevangelium Jacobi. English. II. Title.
BS2860.J3H63 1997
229'.8—dc21   97-28452
                                                                                  CIP

ISBN: 1-56975-079-3

Printed in the United States by R.R. Donnelley & Sons

10 9 8 7 6 5 4 3 2 1

Cover Design: Big Fish
Interior Design: David Wells

Distributed in the United States by Publishers Group West, in Canada by Raincoast Books, and in Great Britain and Europe by World Leisure Marketing.

CONTENTS

INTRODUCTION

∽ i ∾

In the entire history of the world, there are few women as famous as Mary. Known to Christians for two thousand years as the mother of Jesus, she is also portrayed as the ultimate symbol of purity. Today, the veneration of Mary is stronger than ever. Five million people a year visit France to bathe in the waters of Lourdes, whose healing effects are attributed to her powers. Two *billion* Hail Marys are said every day.

Since 1993, millions of Roman Catholics have petitioned Pope John Paul II to proclaim a new dogma that would effectively add Mary to the Holy Trinity. Among her supporters are forty-two cardinals and more than four hundred bishops. The petitions to Rome have arrived from more than one hundred and fifty countries around the world. Mary, as *A History of God* author Karen Armstrong says, "is a major celebrity."

But who was this woman? Most of what we know about her derives from the New Testament. When it comes to the biography of Mary, however, the New Testament raises more questions than it answers. The Gospels of Matthew and Luke grant her a few hundred words; those of Mark and John, perhaps a hundred. But nearly two thousand years after their scant accounts were set down, Mary remains one of the most important female symbols in the world. As the twentieth century comes to a close, the Marian cult is one of the most powerful and divisive issues in Christianity. Given short shrift in the New Testament, periodically exalted and then demoted by the Church, she has been adapted, interpreted and mythicized—but consistently venerated over the centuries by everyday Christians.

Despite the New Testament's lack of detail concerning Mary's birth, maidenhood and eventual marriage to Joseph, many episodes from her life decorate churches around the world and have become well known to her admirers. Giotto di Bondone, considered the greatest artist in pre-Renaissance Italy, painted a fresco in the Arena Chapel in Padua that portrays a sequence of events in Mary's life unknown to the New Testament. He shows her mother Anne and father Joachim (who do not appear at all in the New Testament) being told of her forthcoming birth. This scene, reminiscent of the later Annunciation of Jesus' birth to Mary, is accompanied by a painting of Mary being born. Giotto continues his sequence of biographical portraits with a scene of Mary as a young virgin being presented to the elders in the Temple. Even more dramatically, he portrays her marriage to Joseph.

Similarly, the Chora Monastery in Constantinople (Istanbul) contains mosaics that capture a cycle of over twenty events from Mary's life, most of which do not occur in the New Testament. During the fifth and later centuries, these events became the basis of feasts to honor Mary. It is a well-known fact that Pulcheria, the sister of the Roman Emperor Theodosius II, devoted her life to the Virgin Mary. Using details of Mary's life to support her campaign, she succeeded at the Council of Ephesus in 431 A.D. in having Mary declared the Mother of God.

Like Giotto in Italy, mosaic artists in ancient Turkey, and painters scattered throughout the Roman Empire, Pulcheria derived much of her information not from the

This image of Mary, a mosaic entitled "Head of the Virgin," resides in the Hagia Sophia. One of the East's most spectacular examples of religious architecture, the cathedral in Istanbul is dedicated to Mary.

Gospels of Matthew, Mark, Luke and John, but from a then-popular but now almost totally unknown narrative entitled "The Infancy Gospel of James." Probably written in the second century, it was circulated among Christians for hundreds of years.

Purportedly written by James, the brother of Jesus, this ancient biography begins with the period before Mary's birth. In a compelling narrative it explains how an angel informs her parents that they will bear a special child. It tells of Mary's upbringing in the temple and her marriage to Joseph. The story follows the couple's trials as they face the difficulties resulting from Mary's virginal conception, then provides a unique account of Jesus' birth in which he is born not in a stable but a cave.

At roughly the same time that Pulcheria was glorifying Mary, the great biblical scholar Jerome was translating the Bible from its original Greek and Hebrew into the Latin version that would become universal to Western Catholicism for the next fifteen hundred years. Jerome did not regard the Infancy Gospel of James as orthodox, and the story was later included in a papal list of proscribed works.

As a result, the Gospel was largely forgotten in the West until the dawn of the Renaissance. But the devotional art it had helped to inspire continued to adorn newly built churches. The worship of Mary spread, and in time some of the world's most triumphant religious architecture—Chartres and Nôtre Dame cathedrals in France, the Hagia Sofia in Istanbul, and Rome's Santa Maria Maggiore—would be dedicated to the Mother of God. A movement spurred in part by a mysterious Gospel rejected by the Catholic Church had become one of the most vital aspects of Christianity.

ii

While the New Testament focuses on Mary and Joseph in the context of the birth of Jesus, the Infancy Gospel of James begins years earlier by describing the plight of an elderly couple named Joachim and Anne. Though prosperous and prominent, they are childless, a condition not acceptable to the society of their time. As a result, Joachim is publicly chastised and his offerings to God are rejected by the priests.

Eventually he learns that he alone among the good people of Israel has no children, and he decides to retreat into the wilderness to fast and pray until God tells him why he is childless. His wife Anne is similarly blamed by her own slave for being barren. Stricken with sorrow, she sits in her garden only to be further reminded of her barrenness by the fruitfulness of everything around her.

"The Annunciation to Anne and Joachim" captures a scene from the Infancy Gospel of James that does not appear in the New Testament. An angel informs Mary's parents that after years of barrenness, a sacred child will be born to them.

In a scene that Giotto would eventually paint on a church wall in Italy, an angel hears Anne's lament and informs her that she will bear a child who will be known throughout the world. In the desert, Joachim is likewise told that his prayers have been heard. Overcome with joy, Anne vows to dedicate her child to God and Joachim rushes from the desert to be reunited with his wife. The child, of course, is Mary.

After Mary's birth, Anne transforms the baby's bedroom into a sanctuary where nothing unclean can touch her. On the young girl's first birthday, the priests bless her. Then when she is three, her parents fulfill their vow and present Mary to the priests in the Temple in Jerusalem. There she spends the rest of her childhood, fed by the hand of an angel.

None of this appears in the New Testament. Even when the Infancy Gospel begins to overlap with material from Matthew and Luke, it tells a very different and much more detailed story. At the age of twelve, Mary is about to become a woman, and hence a threat to the Temple's purity. Having sought divine guidance, the high priest is instructed to summon all the widowers of Israel. Each is to bring his staff; a sign will determine which of the suitors is to receive her as his ward.

Among the widowers is a man named Joseph, who in this account is described as an old man with grown sons. A dove flies out from Joseph's staff and perches on his head, indicating that he is chosen to receive Mary. Joseph takes Mary home, but being a carpenter he soon leaves to go and build houses, trusting in God to protect her.

Together with other virgins, Mary is asked by the high priest to spin thread for a new temple veil. While drawing water from a well, Mary hears a voice; terrified, she hurries home to her spinning. The voice is that of an angel, who addresses her again, saying that she has found favor with God and will conceive by means of his word. In a scene very similar to the Annunciation in the New Testament, she is told that the child will be divine and that she is to call him Jesus.

Mary finishes her spinning and takes her thread to the high priest, then goes to stay with her relative Elizabeth, who is herself pregnant with the future John the Baptist. The details of their meeting are similar to those in the Gospel of Luke, complete with their greetings to one another and an incident in which the unborn John leaps for joy in his mother's womb.

Mary returns to Joseph's house after three months, and after three more months he rejoins her there. Once again the story begins to diverge from the biblical account, adding biographical anecdotes that would inspire devotional artworks but never become part of the New Testament.

On finding Mary pregnant, Joseph initially blames himself for failing to protect her. Then he rebukes Mary sharply and, despite her claims of innocence, resolves to divorce her. But that night, Joseph has a dream in which an angel tells him that Mary is pregnant by the Holy Spirit and that he is to name the child Jesus. Obedient to

Diverging widely from the Biblical accounts of Mary and Joseph,
the Infancy Gospel describes how Joseph initially turns against Mary
upon learning of her pregnancy. After vowing to divorce her,
he has a dream in which an angel explains the child's divine origins.

the angel's message, Joseph abandons his thoughts of divorce.

A major crisis soon develops when a visitor realizes that Mary is pregnant and tells the high priest that Joseph has violated the virgin in his care. Summoning Joseph and Mary to answer this charge, the priest hears their denials. In a dramatic confrontation unknown to the New Testament, the priest refuses to believe them and orders Joseph to return Mary to the Temple. Joseph weeps at the thought of losing her and the high priest partially relents by sending them into the wilderness to test their honesty. When they return unharmed, the priest realizes that they are innocent and publicly exonerates the couple.

From this point, James is similar in some respects to the birth stories of Matthew and Luke, but a close reading reveals many significant departures from the canonical accounts. Joseph and Mary heed Emperor Augustus' call for a census and head for Bethlehem, as in the Lukan account. But the author of the Infancy Gospel of James expands the narrative considerably. He adds a speech by Joseph detailing how Mary should be described for the census. There's a conversation between Joseph and Mary while they travel. Most importantly, they stop before reaching Bethlehem so that Mary can deliver her child not in a manger but in a cave. Also included is a miraculous vision that Joseph experiences at the moment of Jesus' birth in which time stands still—clouds and birds are frozen in the air, and men and animals remain motionless on the ground.

Where Luke tells of shepherds arriving from their fields, the Infancy Gospel has two midwives who visit the cave where Mary has given birth. Skeptical of the claim of one midwife that a virgin has given birth, the second midwife performs a physical examination and confirms that the child has indeed been born to a virgin.

As Joseph, Mary and the infant Jesus are preparing to leave for Bethlehem, the Magi arrive at the cave in search of the newborn king of the Judeans. Here, the Infancy Gospel's guiding star and the gifts of gold, frankincense and myrrh recall the Gospel of Matthew. The Magi do not report the child's whereabouts to Herod. As in the Bible, Herod's fear and rage lead him to order the murder of children under two in order to ensure the removal of his royal rival.

Then the Infancy Gospel departs once again from the traditional story: Instead of having Jesus escape Herod's soldiers by means of Joseph's flight to Egypt, his life is saved when Mary wraps him in swaddling cloths and hides him in a manger.

Surprisingly, the closing scene deals not with Mary and Jesus but with John the Baptist. His mother Elizabeth, terrified by Herod's murderous decree, flees to the hills with her baby. John's father Zechariah, who is serving at the time as a priest in the Temple, refuses to tell Herod's agents where his wife and child have gone. He pays for his silence with his life.

✍ iii ✍

O f the many mysteries surrounding the Infancy Gospel, none is more intriguing than the question of who could have written it. Like detectives following a trail nearly two thousand years old, historians have puzzled long and hard over clues contained in the text. Foremost is what the writer says about himself.

The author of the Infancy Gospel of James closes with an autobiographical note. "Now I, James, am the one who wrote this account at the time when an uproar arose in Jerusalem at the death of Herod." Were that true—if the story's source really was Jesus' half-brother James—the Infancy Gospel would be extraordinarily important. It would in fact be an eyewitness account told by someone who knew both Jesus and Mary intimately and who was writing around the time of Jesus' birth. This would mean that the Infancy Gospel predated the four Gospels of the New Testament by seventy to one hundred years.

But the author's statement is cast into doubt by a close reading of his own document. As we analyze the text, it becomes clear that the Gospel of James draws upon those of Matthew and Luke, and not the other way around. First of all, it answers a question that would not even have come up until after Matthew and Luke set down their accounts.

In Matthew's birth story, King Herod orders the murder of all the young children around Bethlehem and Joseph flees to Egypt to save Jesus. Luke tells us that Elizabeth, the mother of John the Baptist, gave birth only a few months before Mary. Individually, the stories present no conflict. Together, they raise the question of how the infant John survived the slaughter.

The Infancy Gospel attributed to James takes pains to answer the question, explaining that John was saved when his mother took him off to the hills to hide, and that Zechariah sacrificed his own life by refusing to reveal his son's whereabouts.

The entire question of Herod's rampage and John's remarkable escape was first raised in Matthew and Luke. Most historians believe that the Gospels of Matthew and

While the painting of "Joseph's Dream" (page 11) derives from the Infancy Gospel, this portrayal of The Flight into Egypt comes from the Gospel of Matthew. Both artworks are part of the Menologian of Basil II (ca. 986) series found in Constantinople.

Luke were written around 80 or 90 A.D. But Jesus' half-brother James died in 62 A.D., twenty or thirty years before those Gospels were written. He would never have seen either Matthew's or Luke's Gospel.

Who, then, did write the Infancy Gospel of James? Detective work pursued down so many centuries is unlikely to yield any tidy conclusions. From the way he handles the story of John the Baptist, it is clear that the author wrote in reaction to the Gospels of Matthew and Luke; therefore the story could not have been set down before the end of the first century. The earliest known manuscript containing the Infancy Gospel of James is the Bodmer Papyrus V, which dates from the early fourth century—so it wasn't written later than that.

Within those time boundaries, we can begin to locate the author, or at least the time when he was writing, by tracing the story's influence on other Christian literature. That the Infancy Gospel was known in the early third century is clear from the writings of Clement of Alexandria and his pupil Origen (who died around 253 A.D.). Clement speaks of the midwife who proclaimed Mary to be a virgin. Origen, who became one of the most important biblical scholars of the early church, identifies Jesus' brothers as Joseph's sons from a previous marriage. These references suggest that the Gospel was composed before the end of the second century. Beyond that, the clues grow more ambiguous: Around the middle of the second century, Justin Martyr (an early Christian saint who died around 165 A.D.) referred to the birth of Jesus as having occurred in a cave. It's a point of agreement with the Infancy Gospel, and similarities of style suggest that Justin drew upon that record. But the reference is vague, the connection obscure; we can't confidently take the Gospel's origins back to the early second century. All the evidence allows us is a date before that century's end.

Which does not get us far in the pursuit of the author himself.

Hidden behind his pseudonym, the Infancy Gospel's author still reveals something of himself in the narrative. His confusion about the geographic relation of Bethlehem to Jerusalem and Judea suggests that he was a stranger to Palestine. (Scholars have tentatively placed him in Syria or Egypt, but this can only be educated guesswork.). More important is what his document reveals about his literary ability and training. "James" writes in a simple, lucid style appropriate to his story of innocence and birth. His expressive power becomes clear when he describes the poignant lament of Mary's mother Anne over her barrenness. His education shows in his familiarity with the Old Testament, which he mines for historical analogies, turns of phrase, and information about Jewish life and practices. Obviously, he is familiar with the Gospels of Matthew and Luke. And a solid grounding in rhetoric is clear in his use of antithesis, comparison and dialogue as well as in his adoption of an "encomium," or tribute, to help structure his narrative.

In the end, the author of the Infancy Gospel leaves us in the dark as to his true identity. But his narrative does tell us that he was a well-educated man writing perhaps in second-century Syria or Egypt; someone with a sense of literary drama, a passion for the story of Mary's life, and the ability to write a complex story with a compelling plot and a tightly woven theme.

✺ iv ✺

Even if it is impossible to determine exactly who wrote the Infancy Gospel, we should be able to figure out why he wrote it. The first thing to look at is the central theme, Mary's purity, which is a constant thread that unifies the characters and entwined plots of the entire Gospel. It is most obvious, of course, in the assertion that Mary was a virgin before and after the birth of Jesus. It is also seen when her mother Anne transforms the bedroom into a sanctuary and has Mary associate only with undefiled daughters of the Hebrews. Mary's childhood years are spent in the Temple, where she is fed by the hand of an angel.

When she moves into Joseph's house as a young maiden, he immediately departs, entrusting her to divine protection and removing even the possibility of sexuality. It's also significant that Joseph is characterized as an old man who has no interest in Mary as a woman. After he goes away, she spends her time with other virgins in the virtuous task of spinning thread.

Given this description, it is difficult to imagine anyone more pure than Mary; and here lies the main clue to the author's purpose. This unbroken emphasis on purity could lead us to suspect, as many scholars do, that the Gospel's function was that of a defense. During the second century, when the Christian movement was composed of many sects, Mary was the object of numerous attacks both from within the church and outside it. Critics claimed it was her poverty and low status, not her devotion, that made her spin for a living. Some even charged that she had been convicted of adultery, going so far as to name a Roman soldier who they claimed was Jesus' father.

The possibility that the Infancy Gospel was written in reaction to such stories is supported to some extent by the text. The test of Mary and Joseph that leads to their public exoneration by the high priest and the midwife's physical examination of Mary to confirm her virginity support this interpretation. There's also the emphasis on Joachim's and Anne's wealth and prominence, which undermines claims that Mary was poor; and the idea that she was spinning thread for a Temple veil could be an attempt to refute the assertion that she spun to earn a living.

But investigating more closely, it becomes obvious that this is a false lead. Apology shouldn't be ruled out entirely in our interpretation of the Infancy Gospel, but it doesn't explain the Gospel as a whole; and the passages that do seem like apologies can be interpreted in other ways. Spinning, for example, is usually associated with womanly virtue in ancient texts.

"The Virgin Receiving the Skein of Purple Wool" is portrayed in this early-twelfth-century miniature. It is among a series of artworks from the Vatican Library, "Homilies of the Monk James," that illustrate scenes from a Gospel rejected by the Catholic Church.

As a matter of fact, if we examine the ancient texts that were being written shortly after the time of Mary and Jesus, we find pretty clear evidence of what the author intended. In the Hellenistic culture that pervaded the Roman Empire during the second century A.D., a specific literary style was used by writers to praise their subjects. Called an encomium, it followed strict rules of composition. These rules were taught in the schools of the ancient world. A "textbook" called a *Progymnasmata* explained this course in composition.

The *Progymnasmata* contained fourteen exercises in composition, beginning with easy ones, such as fables and mythological stories, and moving on to complex essays. Midway through the series was the encomium. Students learned to write one by following an outline and developing a style appropriate to the form.

An encomium, they were told, includes an introduction; details of the person's family background, childhood and adult life; a list of deeds illustrating their virtues; a comparison with someone of equal or greater virtue; and a conclusion, usually in the form of a prayer. To fill in this formal outline, students were advised to tell of the person's birth (especially if it involved miracles) and to organize their subject's good deeds around the four cardinal virtues of justice, self-control, courage and wisdom. It was also important to include details about the fame both of subjects and their descendants.

If all of this is beginning to sound familiar, that's because the Infancy Gospel of James is clearly an "encomium," a special tribute to Mary written by an author whose name we do not know but whose motives will become clear as we look at how closely he adheres to each of the characteristics of an encomium.

• FAMILY BACKGROUND, traditionally the first section of an encomium, addresses the subject's race, nationality, parents and ancestors. In the Infancy Gospel, Mary's heritage makes her worthy of praise even before she is born. The opening words, "According to the records of the twelve tribes of Israel," identify her race.

Her parents are portrayed as prosperous, prominent and pious; in narrating their attempts to have a child, the author refers to Abraham and Sarah, Mary's illustrious ancestors. Miracles attend her conception, and Mary's parents are informed by angels that Anne is at last pregnant. Anne in turn prophesies that her child will be "talked about all over the world."

• UPBRINGING: The next two chapters are devoted to Mary's extraordinary childhood. Anne raises Mary in

As Mary's popularity increased over the centuries, artists throughout Europe and the Near East drew ideas and inspiration from the stories told in *The Infancy Gospel of James*. In the case of painters like Giotto di Bondone, whose early-Rennaissance images from the Arena Chapel in Padua appear here, they presented a complete cycle of events from Mary's life. Though most European works were commissioned by the Catholic Church, the artists found little Mary material in the New Testament and instead used subject matter from a text that was banned by the Church. In the portrait above, Mary's father is expelled from the temple. The images that follow capture other scenes from the Infancy Gospel.

THE ANNUNCIATION TO ANNA Suddenly a messenger of the Lord appeared to her and said to her: "Anne, Anne, the Lord God has heard your prayer. You will conceive and give birth, and your child will be talked about all over the world."

And Anne said, "As the Lord God lives, whether I give birth to a boy or a girl, I'll offer it as a gift to the Lord my God, and it will serve him its whole life."

THE VISION OF JOACHIM Two messengers reported to her:
"Look, your husband Joachim is coming with his flocks. You see,
a messenger of the Lord had come down to Joachim and said,
'Joachim, Joachim, the Lord God has heard your prayer. Get
down from there. Look, your wife Anne is pregnant.'"

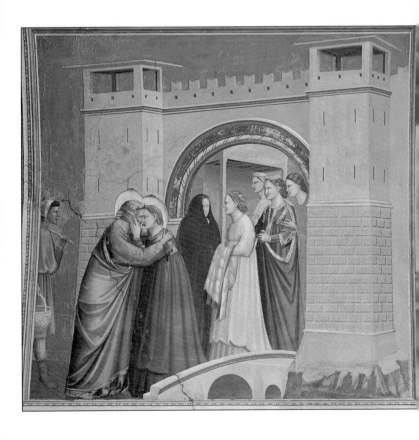

THE MEETING AT THE GOLDEN GATE And so Joachim was coming with his flocks, while Anne stood at the gate. Then she spotted Joachim approaching with his flocks and rushed out and threw her arms around his neck and said, "Now I know that the Lord God has blessed me greatly. This widow is no longer a widow, and I, once childless, am now pregnant!"

THE BIRTH OF THE VIRGIN And so her pregnancy came to term, and in the ninth month Anne gave birth. And she said to the midwife, "Is it a boy or girl?"

And her midwife said, "A girl."

And Anne said, "I have been greatly honored this day."

And she offered her breast to the child and gave her the name Mary.

THE PRESENTATION OF THE VIRGIN IN THE TEMPLE The priest welcomed her, kissed her, and blessed her: "The Lord God has exalted your name among all generations. In you the Lord will disclose his redemption to the people of Israel during the last days."

And he sat her down on the third step of the altar, and the Lord God showered favor on her. And she danced, and the whole house of Israel loved her.

THE PRESENTATION OF THE RODS Joseph, too, threw down his carpenter's ax and left for the meeting. When they had all gathered, they went to the high priest with their staffs. After the high priest had collected everyone's staff, he entered the temple and began to pray.

THE BETROTHAL OF THE VIRGIN "Joseph, Joseph," the high priest said, "you've been chosen by lot to take the virgin of the Lord into your care and protection."

And so out of fear Joseph took her into his care and protection. He said to her, "Mary, I've gotten you from the temple of the Lord, but now I'm leaving you at home. I'm going away to build houses, but I'll come back to you. The Lord will protect you."

the purest environment, transforming her bedroom into a sanctuary and not allowing Mary to touch the ground. On Mary's first birthday, celebrated with a great banquet and attended by elders and scholars, the high priest prophesies greatness and asks that the child's name be on people's lips forever.

Mary's upbringing becomes even more extraordinary when Joachim and Anne fulfill their vow and present their child to the priests in the Temple, where she lives for the next nine years, being fed from the hand of an angel.

"The Presentation of the Virgin in the Temple" comes from a chapel in Serbia, the Church of Sts. Joachim and Anne, that was named after Mary's parents. Here they are portrayed on the left while the group of maidens in the center presents Mary to the high priest.

• ADULT PURSUITS: When Mary becomes a young woman, "James" begins the third part of his encomium, telling of her important work spinning thread for a new Temple veil and portraying her as able and responsible. He also describes how Mary learns of an infinitely more important adult responsibility when an angel tells her that she will bear a son who will save his people from their sins. Acknowledging her ability and willingness to assume the challenge, Mary replies, "Here I am."

• VIRTUE is the encomium's most important element, and Mary's exemplary behavior receives ample attention. Chapters thirteen through twenty-two are devoted to the discussion of her purity or, in the language of the cardinal virtues, her self-control.

When Mary is six months pregnant, she adamantly insists—first in the face of Joseph's disbelief and then before the high priest—that she practiced this self-control during Joseph's absence. To both she maintains that she has had sex with no man, and her insistence is upheld when an angel informs Joseph in a dream that Mary's child is of the holy spirit.

Shortly after the trial that tests and affirms her virtue, Mary accompanies Joseph to Bethlehem. While the Gospel of Matthew portrays her as fleeing to Egypt to escape King Herod, the author of the Infancy Gospel gives her an opportunity to demonstrate one more virtue—courage—when she saves the baby Jesus by hiding him in a manger.

This is the last we hear of Mary and her family. The story turns to Elizabeth and Zechariah, the parents of John the Baptist. This shift has puzzled many scholars, some of whom suspect that these passages were written by a different author and added later. But if we accept that the Infancy Gospel of James is an encomium, we realize that the author has simply learned his lessons well: He has included one of the final elements, a comparison of the person being praised with someone of equal or greater virtue. Thus Zechariah's extraordinary courage in defending his son, an act of valor that costs him his life, provides a positive comparison to Mary's courage in protecting Jesus.

Further recalling his schooling, the author closes by praising God. "Grace will be with all those who fear the Lord. Amen." From beginning to end, "James" has followed each of the standard instructions for writing an encomium, fitting his biography of Mary very neatly into one of the most popular genres of the age.

သ V ယ

So far our investigation into the Infancy Gospel has revealed that it comes from the second century. We have also determined that the work was not intended to rebut Mary's critics but as a biography filled with praise.

Among the questions that remain is why the author emphasizes Mary's purity so excessively. In the Gospel of Luke, Mary is commended instead for her obedience. Chastity doesn't seem to be much of an issue in any of the New Testament accounts.

One clue here is that the author of the Infancy Gospel is seeking to answer a question that is implicit throughout his narrative: Why was Mary chosen to be the mother of the son of God? The fact that he settles on her purity as the solution reveals a distinctly second-century perspective on chastity. In the early Roman Empire, self-control was widely admired. The quality had long been among the cardinal virtues, and literary works from the second century—whether pastoral poems, satires, philosophical treatises or romances—often see sexual abstinence as the most important of all the virtues and emphasize it as strongly as does the Infancy Gospel.

Sexual self-control was recommended for both men and women. *The Ephesian Tale*, by Xenophon (a contemporary of the Infancy Gospel's author), tells of Habrocomes and Anthia, who remain chaste in the face of separation and temptation. When they are finally reunited, they recount the story of their trials and reaffirm their virtue. (Habrocomes refers to his self-control as his *syntrophos*—a household slave purchased in infancy who grows up as a companion to the master's son. The metaphor personifies the quality of self-control as an early, close and abiding concern.)

So in the Infancy Gospel, Joseph doubts Mary when she claims that she hasn't had sex with anyone, and the high priest questions Joseph's integrity as well, forcing both of them to undergo tests of purity. Seeing them pass the tests would been very satisfying to a second-century reader, and the idea that Mary was chosen for a divine role because of her extraordinary purity would have been eminently plausible.

Another element that places the Infancy Gospel some-what later than those of Matthew, Mark, Luke and John is the way in which it handles the entire question of Jesus' identity. Early chronicles of his life dealt with Jesus' death and resurrection rather than his birth.

Paul, writing his letters in the 50s A.D., said only that Jesus was "born of a woman, born under the law." Nothing extraordinary about the birth appears in his writings; and he didn't even mention that Mary is the mother.

Written about twenty years later, the Gospel of Mark focused more closely on the story of Jesus' life. But even here he came into the picture as a young man, ready for baptism. His earlier life was not discussed, although Mark did identify Jesus' mother as Mary and named four brothers—James, Joses, Jude and Simon—as well as an unspecified number of sisters. He also referred to Jesus as the son of God at three prominent points in his narrative—at the beginning, during the baptism and at the cross—and in doing so initiated a strong interest in the circumstances of Jesus' conception and birth.

The authors of the Gospels of Matthew and Luke, writing around 80 or 90 A.D., used the Gospel of Mark as one of their sources. But both Matthew and Luke begin their narratives with Jesus' birth, probably in an

Mary's purity, a theme that predominates throughout the Infancy Gospel and also appears in the New Testament, is strikingly illuminated in this fifteenth-century painting by the Florentine Renaissance portraitist Sandro Botticelli.

attempt to explain how it was that Jesus came to be the son of God. So it appears that interest in Jesus' birth arose after 70 A.D. This is evident from the inconsistencies between the stories told in Matthew and Luke. They provide different accounts of the movements of Joseph and Mary, of the secondary characters, and of events and chronology. What this means is that at the time they were writing, there was no standard account of the birth; they were doing what they had been taught to do when writing a narrative—telling a plausible story.

This line of reasoning casts more doubt, if any is needed, on the Infancy Gospel's alleged date of 4 B.C. Further, the Infancy Gospel answers many questions raised by the Gospels of Matthew and Luke. What was Joseph's precise relationship to Mary? Did Jesus have real brothers and sisters? Why was Mary chosen to bear the son of God? The Infancy Gospel's revisionist characterization of Joseph as an old man with grown children from a previous marriage, and its overarching assertion of Mary's purity, support the proposition that Jesus was of divine origin.

Thus, by the end of the first century, the entirety of Jesus' life had become the subject of considerable and sustained Christian reflection. In the second century, attention turned increasingly to the marvels that attended his birth, and especially to the lineage, life and virtuous deeds of his mother Mary.

✧ vi ✧

The Infancy Gospel of James represents the culmination of these early developments in Christian thought, but its most important historical and cultural influences were yet to be felt. To appreciate the Gospel's power, we need to look at how it spread in the divided Roman Empire.

By 200 A.D., political and economic blight had set in throughout the Roman Empire, which had grown to an ungovernable size. Its rule was further destabilized in the third century by border wars and invasion by barbarians. Perhaps one hundred years after the Infancy Gospel was set down, Emperor Diocletian divided Rome's immense holdings into two great territories—the Western Empire, centered in Rome, and the Eastern Empire, ruled from Constantinople.

The Infancy Gospel was fully accepted in the Eastern Empire. Its broad popularity is evident from the variety of languages into which the text was translated over the centuries—Syriac, Armenian, Georgian, Ethiopic and Coptic. Mary's story became profoundly influential in Eastern Christianity, thanks in large part to the faith of Pulcheria, the aristocratic citizen of fifth-century Constantinople who was mentioned earlier.

Though the Infancy Gospel of James had been in circulation from at least as early as the mid-second century, interest in Mary had remained abstract. Over these early centuries, it had focused largely on the issue of her virginity and on aspects of her life specific to the birth of Jesus. Then Pulcheria, sister of Emperor Theodosius II, dedicated her life to Mary. Modeling her behavior on what she knew of the Virgin, Pulcheria took a public vow of chastity and launched a crusade to establish Mary as the focal point of piety in Constantinople.

She built three churches to Mary, gathered Marian relics (her shroud and an icon said to have been painted by the apostle Luke), and in various ways sought to incorporate Mary's worship into the religious ceremonies of the Byzantine capital. At the Council of Ephesus in 431 A.D., Pulcheria argued for and achieved Mary's official recognition as *Theotokos*, the Mother of God.

As a result, churches throughout the Byzantine Empire were dedicated to Mary, or to her parents Joachim and Anne. Assigned to decorate these churches, artists turned to the Infancy Gospel of James for details of Mary's story that they could render in paint and mosaic. A series of twenty events from Mary's life—starting with the scene in the Infancy Gospel where her father's offerings are rejected and ending with the birth of Jesus— became standard subjects. In addition, Mary's birth and her presentation at the Temple came to be celebrated as holy feast days and were widely represented in devotional art.

The Infancy Gospel's direct influence on this genre shows clearly in a sixth-century ivory plaque, probably Syrian, in the collection of the Hermitage Museum of St. Petersburg. The garden scene on the plaque has an angel telling Anne that she will soon become pregnant. A tree in the background, its branches alive with birds, conforms closely to the Gospel's description of the garden in which Anne laments her barrenness. The corresponding heavenly annunciation to Joachim appears in a twelfth-century mosaic in the Church of the Dormition, located in Daphni just outside Athens. The name "Joachim," written above the seated man, and the angel's words, "Your prayer has been answered," recall the Infancy Gospel's account of the incident.

The Hermitage Museum in St. Petersburg, Russia, is home to this sixth-century ivory plaque. The tree filled with birds reflects the garden setting in which Anne first laments over her barrenness and then rejoices upon being told of the forthcoming birth of Mary.

Some of these representations could as easily derive from the canonical accounts, for the Infancy Gospel drew upon them for parts of its narrative. But again and again, significant details make it clear that their creators turned to the second-century document, and not the Gospels of Matthew or Luke, as their primary source.

The final event in the Marian cycle is the birth of Jesus. Here again, artists could use the imagery of the canonical Gospels as well as that of the Infancy Gospel, and indeed many examples reflect the canonical versions. Another mosaic at Daphni shows the infant Jesus in a manger with angels announcing his birth to shepherds and Matthew's star casting its beam. But other features—a cave as the setting for the birth, with Joseph outside, and starlight that shines directly down upon the infant's head—are pure Infancy Gospel.

The Gospel was known in the Western Empire as well. A hymn to Mary, partially preserved on papyrus, recently came to light in Egypt. Composed in Latin in the third or fourth century, the manuscript refers to episodes in Mary's life that clearly have their source in the Infancy Gospel: Anne's lament, Joachim and Anne turning Mary over to the Temple priests, Mary being nourished by angels, Jesus' birth in a cave.

But the Gospel's influence in the Latin-speaking West was diminished by scholarly opposition to its contents, especially to the mention of Jesus' half-brothers. In the late fourth century, the biblical scholar Jerome interpreted Matthew's and Mark's references to Jesus' siblings, which undercut Jesus' divinity and Mary's virginity, to mean Jesus' cousins. He strongly objected to the Infancy Gospel's assertion that Jesus' brothers were children of Joseph's earlier marriage.

Jerome—secretary to Pope Saint Damasus, colleague of Saint Augustine, and the man who undertook the monumental translation of the Bible into Latin from its original Greek and Hebrew—wielded enormous influence in the world of Christian scholarship. His rejection of the Infancy Gospel effectively blocked its spread in the West. The sixth-century Gelasian Decree, a list of acceptable and unacceptable books, put the Infancy Gospel of James in the latter category. As a result, no Latin manuscripts of the Gospel exist; it effectively disappeared in the West for the next thousand years.

But the story of the Infancy Gospel of James has never followed a direct line. Just as it entered Christian consciousness through the back door, influencing devotional art at the same time it was being rejected by the

Church, so it remained alive in manuscript form by means of a document known as the Gospel of Pseudo-Matthew. Possibly dating from as long ago as the seventh century and circulated throughout the Western Empire, Pseudo-Matthew begins by recounting (with some variations) the story told in the Infancy Gospel, continues with a lengthy account of the Flight into Egypt, and goes on to tell a number of tales about Jesus as a child. Letters accompanying the document assert that the Apostle Matthew composed it in Hebrew and that Jerome translated it into Latin—a fine irony, since Pseudo-Matthew claims that Jesus' brothers were the children of Joseph.

At any rate, the boundaries of Eastern and Western culture were porous. Through Pseudo-Matthew and other means, awareness of the story contained in the Infancy Gospel of James leaked into European consciousness, and the cycle of scenes from Mary's life became well represented in European art.

One of the most important examples of its influence is a series of frescoes by the great Florentine painter Giotto di Bondone, in the Arena Chapel at Padua. Giotto is celebrated for his departure from the traditional Byzantine forms and his ability to create a powerful style of his own. Interestingly, Giotto's scene of Anne's and Joachim's meeting at the gate includes some details peculiar to the Gospel of Pseudo-Matthew. For the most part, however, the Padua frescoes depict the same cycle of events that adorns many Eastern churches: the expulsion of Joachim from the Temple, the birth of Mary, the handing over of the widowers' staffs to the high priest, and so on.

Traditions are commingled, sources contradict one another, meanings grow blurred, rituals change in content, old stories are reshaped into new forms, revised by fiat, and translated into languages that go extinct: that's history. In the case of the Infancy Gospel of James, this confusing pattern is even more difficult to discern. Received very differently in the East and the West, it had a profound effect—despite its official rejection in Rome—upon artists and common people throughout the Roman Empire. Ultimately, it is a vital work of early Christian literature and a remarkable example of the unpredictable routes along which history sometimes leads its most venerable treasures.

Mary
in the
New
Testament

While most people believe that there is ample information about Mary in the Bible, the number of New Testament references to her actually total fewer than two dozen. Many of the details that form the folklore of Mary come from other sources, particularly the Infancy Gospel of James. As startling evidence of how little Mary material actually appears in the canonical Gospels, here are the relevant passages from the Bible.

NOW THE BIRTH OF JESUS THE MESSIAH TOOK PLACE in this way. When his mother Mary had been engaged to Joseph, but before they lived together, she was found to be with child from the Holy Spirit. Her husband Joseph, being a righteous man and unwilling to expose her to public disgrace, planned to dismiss her quietly. But just when he had resolved to do this, an angel of the Lord appeared to him in a dream and said, "Joseph, son of David, do not be afraid to take Mary as your wife, for the child conceived in her is from the Holy Spirit. She will bear a son, and you are to name him Jesus, for he will save his people from their sins."

All this took place to fulfill what had been spoken by the Lord through the prophet: "Look, the virgin shall conceive and bear a son, and they shall name him Emmanuel," which means, "God is with us." When Joseph awoke from sleep, he did as the angel of the Lord commanded him; he took her as his wife, but had no marital relations with her until she had borne a son; and he named him Jesus.

O N ENTERING THE HOUSE, THE WISE MEN SAW THE child with Mary his mother; and they knelt down and paid him homage. Then, opening their treasure chests, they offered him gifts of gold, frankincense, and myrrh. And having been warned in a dream not to return to Herod, they left for their own country by another road.

Now after they had left, an angel of the Lord appeared to Joseph in a dream and said, "Get up, take the child and his mother, and flee to Egypt, and remain there until I tell you; for Herod is about to search for the child, to destroy him."

Then Joseph got up, took the child and his mother by night, and went to Egypt, and remained there until the death of Herod. This was to fulfill what had been spoken by the Lord through the prophet, "Out of Egypt I have called my son."

WHILE HE WAS STILL SPEAKING TO THE CROWDS, HIS mother and his brothers were standing outside, wanting to speak to him. Someone told him, "Look, your mother and your brothers are standing outside, wanting to speak to you." But to the one who had told him this, Jesus replied, "Who is my mother, and who are my brothers?" And pointing to his disciples, he said, "Here are my mother and my brothers! For whoever does the will of my Father in heaven is my brother and sister and mother."

MARK 6: 1–3

HE LEFT THAT PLACE AND CAME TO HIS HOMETOWN, and his disciples followed him. On the sabbath he began to teach in the synagogue, and many who heard him were astounded. They said, "Where did this man get all this? What is this wisdom that has been given to him? What deeds of power are being done by his hands! Is not this the carpenter, the son of Mary and brother of James and Joses and Judas and Simon, and are not his sisters here with us?" And they took offense at him.

I N THE SIXTH MONTH THE ANGEL GABRIEL WAS SENT BY God to a town in Galilee called Nazareth, to a virgin engaged to a man whose name was Joseph, of the house of David. The virgin's name was Mary. And he came to her and said, "Greetings, favored one! The Lord is with you." But she was much perplexed by his words and pondered what sort of greeting this might be.

The angel said to her, "Do not be afraid, Mary, for you have found favor with God. And now, you will conceive in your womb and bear a son, and you will call him Jesus. He will be great, and will be called the Son of the Most High, and the Lord God will give to him the throne of his ancestor David. He will reign over the house of Jacob forever, and of his kingdom there will be no end."

Mary said to the angels, "How can this be, since I am a virgin?" The angel said to her, "The Holy Spirit will come upon you, and the power of the Most High will overshadow you; therefore the child to be born will be holy; he will be called Son of God. And now, your relative Elizabeth in her old age has also conceived a son; and this is the sixth month for her who was said to be barren. For nothing will be impossible with God." Then Mary said, "Here am I, the servant of the Lord; let it be with me according to your word." Then the angel departed from her.

In those days Mary set out and went with haste to a Judean town in the hill country, where she entered the house of Zechariah and greeted Elizabeth. When Elizabeth heard Mary's greeting, the child leaped in her womb. And Elizabeth was filled with the Holy Spirit and exclaimed with a loud cry, "Blessed are you among women, and blessed is the fruit of your womb. And why has this happened to me, that the mother of my Lord comes to me? For as soon as I heard the sound of your greeting, the child in my womb leaped for joy. And blessed is she who believed that there would be a fulfillment of what was spoken to her by the Lord."

And Mary said, "My soul magnifies the Lord and my spirit rejoices in God my Savior, for he has looked with favor on the lowliness of his servant. Surely, from now on all generations will call me blessed; for the Mighty One has done great things for me, and holy is his name. His mercy is for those who fear him from generation to generation. He has shown strength with his arm; he has scattered the proud in the thoughts of their hearts. He has brought down the powerful from their thrones, and lifted up the lowly; He has filled the hungry with good things, and sent the rich away empty. He has helped his servant Israel, in remembrance of his mercy, according to the promise he made to our ancestors, to Abraham and to his descendants forever." And Mary remained with her about three months and then returned to her home.

LUKE 2: 5–7

HE WENT TO BE REGISTERED WITH MARY, TO WHOM he was engaged and who was expecting a child. While they were there, the time came for her to deliver her child. And she gave birth to her firstborn son and wrapped him in bands of cloth, and laid him in a manger, because there was no place for them in the inn.

LUKE 2: 15–19

WHEN THE ANGELS HAD LEFT THEM AND GONE INTO heaven, the shepherds said to one another, "Let us go now to Bethlehem and see this thing that has taken place, which the Lord has made known to us." So they went with haste and found Mary and Joseph, and the child lying in the manger. When they saw this, they made known what had been told them about this child; and all who heard it were amazed at what the shepherds told them. But Mary treasured all these words and pondered them in her heart.

"The Marriage Feast at Cana" portrays a scene in Galilee where
Jesus converts water into wine. This is one of the few events
described by the New Testament in which Mary plays a part.

JOHN 2: 1–7

ON THE THIRD DAY THERE WAS A WEDDING IN CANA of Galilee, and the mother of Jesus was there. Jesus and his disciples had also been invited to the wedding. When the wine gave out, the mother of Jesus said to him, "They have no wine." And Jesus said to her, "Woman, what concern is that to you and to me? My hour has not yet come." His mother said to the servants, "Do whatever he tells you." Now standing there were six stone water jars for the Jewish rites of purification, each holding twenty or thirty gallons. Jesus said to them, "Fill the jars with water." And they filled them up to the brim.

JOHN 19: 25–27

AND THAT IS WHAT THE SOLDIERS DID. MEANWHILE, standing near the cross of Jesus were his mother, and his mother's sister, Mary the wife of Clopas, and Mary Magdalene. When Jesus saw his mother and the disciple whom he loved standing beside her, he said to his mother, "Woman, here is your son." Then he said to the disciple, "Here is your mother." And from that hour the disciple took her into his own home.

Infancy
Gospel
of James

↭ 1 ↬

ACCORDING TO THE RECORDS OF THE twelve tribes of Israel, there once was a very rich man named Joachim. He always doubled the gifts he offered to the Lord, and would say to himself, "One gift, representing my prosperity, will be for all the people; the other, offered for forgiveness, will be my sin-offering to the Lord God."

Now the great day of the Lord was approaching, and the people of Israel were offering their gifts. And Reubel confronted Joachim and said, "You're not allowed to offer your gifts first because you haven't produced an Israelite child."

And Joachim became very upset and went to the book of the twelve tribes of the people, saying to himself, "I'm going to check the book of the twelve tribes of Israel to see whether I'm the only one in Israel who hasn't produced a child." And he searched the records and found that all the righteous people in Israel did indeed have children. And he remembered the patriarch Abraham because in his last days the Lord God had given him a son, Isaac.

And so he continued to be very upset and did not see his wife but banished himself to the wilderness and pitched his tent there. And Joachim fasted forty days and forty nights. He would say to himself, "I will not go back for food or drink until the Lord my God visits me. Prayer will be my food and drink."

∽ 2 ∾

NOW HIS WIFE ANNE WAS MOURNING and lamenting on two counts: "I lament my widowhood and I lament my childlessness."

The great day of the Lord approached, however, and Juthine her slave said to her, "How long are you going to humble yourself? Look, the great day of the Lord has arrived, and you're not supposed to mourn. Rather, take this headband which the mistress of the workshop gave to me but which I'm not allowed to wear because I'm your slave and because it bears a royal insignia."

And Anne said, "Get away from me! I won't take it. The Lord God has greatly shamed me. Maybe a trickster has given you this, and you've come to make me share in your sin."

And Juthine the slave replied, "Should I curse you just because you haven't paid any attention to me? The Lord God has made your womb sterile so you won't bear any children for Israel."

Anne, too, became very upset. She took off her mourning clothes, washed her face, and put on her wedding dress. Then in the middle of the afternoon, she went down to her garden to take a walk. She spied a laurel tree and sat down under it. After resting, she prayed to the Lord: "O God of my ancestors, bless me and hear my prayer, just as you blessed our mother Sarah and gave her a son, Isaac."

ꙩ 3 ꙩ

AND ANNE LOOKED UP TOWARD THE sky and saw a nest of sparrows in the laurel tree. And immediately Anne began to lament, saying to herself:

"Poor me! Who gave birth to me? What sort of womb bore me? For I was born under a curse in the eyes of the people of Israel. And I've been reviled and mocked and banished from the temple of the Lord my God.

"Poor me! What am I like? I am not like the birds of the sky, because even the birds of the sky reproduce in your presence, O Lord.

"Poor me! What am I like? I am not like the domestic animals, because even the domestic animals bear young in your presence, O Lord.

"Poor me! What am I like? I am not like the wild animals of the earth, because even the animals of the earth reproduce in your presence, O Lord.

"Poor me! What am I like? I am not like these waters, because even these waters are productive in your presence, O Lord.

"Poor me! What am I like? I am not like this earth, because even the earth produces its crops in season and blesses you, O Lord."

❧ 4 ❧

S UDDENLY A MESSENGER OF THE LORD appeared to her and said to her: "Anne, Anne, the Lord God has heard your prayer. You will conceive and give birth, and your child will be talked about all over the world."

And Anne said, "As the Lord God lives, whether I give birth to a boy or a girl, I'll offer it as a gift to the Lord my God, and it will serve him its whole life."

And right then two messengers reported to her: "Look, your husband Joachim is coming with his flocks. You see, a messenger of the Lord had come down to Joachim and said, 'Joachim, Joachim, the Lord God has heard your prayer. Get down from there. Look, your wife Anne is pregnant.'"

And Joachim went down right away and summoned his shepherds with these instructions: "Bring me ten lambs without spot or blemish, and the ten lambs will be for the Lord God. Also, bring me twelve tender calves, and the twelve calves will be for the priests and the council of elders. Also, one hundred goats, and the one hundred goats will be for the whole people."

And so Joachim was coming with his flocks, while Anne stood at the gate. Then she spotted Joachim approaching with his flocks and rushed out and threw her arms around his neck and said, "Now I know that the Lord God has blessed me greatly. This widow is no longer a widow, and I, once childless, am now pregnant!"

And Joachim rested the first day at home.

৶ 5 ৶

B UT ON THE NEXT DAY, AS HE WAS presenting his gifts, he thought to himself, "If the Lord God has really been merciful to me, the polished disc on the priest's headband will make it clear to me." And so Joachim was presenting his gifts and paying attention to the priest's headband until he went up to the altar of the Lord. And he saw no sin in it. And Joachim said, "Now I know that the Lord God has been merciful to me and has forgiven me all my sins." And he came down from the temple of the Lord acquitted and went back home.

And so her pregnancy came to term, and in the ninth month Anne gave birth. And she said to the midwife, "Is it a boy or girl?"

And her midwife said, "A girl."

And Anne said, "I have been greatly honored this day." Then the midwife put the child to bed.

When, however, the prescribed days were completed, Anne cleansed herself of the flow of blood. And she offered her breast to the infant and gave her the name Mary.

∽ 6 ∾

DAY BY DAY THE INFANT GREW STRONG-er. When she was six months old, her mother put her on the ground to see if she could stand. She walked seven steps and went to her mother's arms. Then her mother picked her up and said, "As the Lord my God lives, you will never walk on this ground again until I take you into the temple of the Lord."

And so she turned her bedroom into a sanctuary and did not permit anything profane or unclean to pass the child's lips. She sent for the undefiled daughters of the Hebrews, and they kept her amused.

Now the child had her first birthday, and Joachim gave a great banquet and invited the high priests, priests, scholars, council of elders, and all the people of Israel. Joachim presented the child to the priests, and they blessed her: "God of our fathers, bless this child and give her a name which will be on the lips of future generations forever."

And everyone said, "So be it. Amen."

He presented her to the high priests, and they blessed her: "Most high God, look on this child and bless her with the ultimate blessing, one which cannot be surpassed."

Her mother then took her up to the sanctuary—the bedroom—and gave her breast to the child. And Anne composed a song for the Lord God:

"I will sing a sacred song to the Lord my God because he has visited me and taken away the disgrace attributed to me by my enemies. The Lord my God has given me the fruit of his righteousness, single yet manifold before him. Who will announce to the sons of Reubel that Anne has a child at her breast? 'Listen, listen, you twelve tribes of Israel: Anne has a child at her breast!' "

Anne made her rest in the bedroom—the sanctuary—and then went out and began serving her guests. When the banquet was over, they left in good spirits and praised the God of Israel.

◊ 7 ◊

M ANY MONTHS PASSED, BUT WHEN THE child reached two years of age, Joachim said, "Let's take her up to the temple of the Lord, so that we can keep the promise we made, or else the Lord will be angry with us and our gift will be unacceptable."

And Anne said, "Let's wait until she is three, so she won't miss her father or mother."

And Joachim agreed: "Let's wait."

When the child turned three years of age, Joachim said, "Let's send for the undefiled Hebrew daughters. Let them each take a lamp and light it, so the child won't turn back and have her heart captivated by things outside the Lord's temple." And this is what they did until the time they ascended to the Lord's temple.

The priest welcomed her, kissed her, and blessed her: "The Lord God has exalted your name among all generations. In you the Lord will disclose his redemption to the people of Israel during the last days."

And he sat her down on the third step of the altar, and the Lord God showered favor on her. And she danced, and the whole house of Israel loved her.

⌘ 8 ⌘

HER PARENTS LEFT FOR HOME MARVEL-
ing and praising and glorifying the Lord
God because the child did not look back at
them. And Mary lived in the temple of the
Lord. She was fed there like a dove, receiving
her food from the hand of a heavenly messenger.

When she turned twelve, however, there
was a meeting of the priests. "Look," they
said, "Mary has turned twelve in the temple
of the Lord. What should we do with her so
she won't pollute the sanctuary of the Lord
our God?" And they said to the high priest,
"You stand at the altar of the Lord. Enter

and pray about her, and we'll do whatever the Lord God discloses to you."

And so the high priest took the vestment with the twelve bells, entered the Holy of Holies, and began to pray about her. And suddenly a messenger of the Lord appeared: "Zechariah, Zechariah, go out and assemble the widowers of the people and have them each bring a staff. She will become the wife of the one to whom the Lord God shows a sign." And so heralds covered the surrounding territory of Judea. The trumpet of the Lord sounded and all the widowers came running.

↶ 9 ↷

JOSEPH, TOO, THREW DOWN HIS CARPEN-
ter's ax and left for the meeting. When
they had all gathered, they went to the high
priest with their staffs. After the high priest
had collected everyone's staff, he entered the
temple and began to pray. When he had finished his prayer, he took the staffs and went
out and began to give them back to each
one. But there was no sign on any of them.
Joseph got the last staff. Suddenly a dove
came out of this staff and perched on Joseph's
head. "Joseph, Joseph," the high priest said,
"you've been chosen by lot to take the virgin
of the Lord into your care and protection."

But Joseph objected: "I already have sons
and I'm an old man; she's only a young woman.

I'm afraid that I'll become the butt of jokes among the people of Israel."

And the high priest responded, "Joseph, fear the Lord your God and remember what God did to Dathan, Abiron, and Kore: the earth was split open and they were all swallowed up because of their objection. So now, Joseph, you ought to take heed so that the same thing won't happen to your family."

And so out of fear Joseph took her into his care and protection. He said to her, "Mary, I've gotten you from the temple of the Lord, but now I'm leaving you at home. I'm going away to build houses, but I'll come back to you. The Lord will protect you."

✺ 10 ✺

MEANWHILE, THERE WAS A COUNCIL of the priests, who agreed: "Let's make a veil for the temple of the Lord."

And the high priest said, "Summon the true virgins for me from the tribe of David." And so the temple assistants left and searched everywhere and found seven. And the high priest then remembered the girl Mary, that she, too, was from the tribe of David and was pure in God's eyes. And so the temple assistants went out and got her.

And they took the maidens into the temple of the Lord. And the high priest said,

"Cast lots for me to decide who'll spin which threads for the veil: the gold, the white, the linen, the silk, the violet, the scarlet, and the true purple."

And the true purple and scarlet threads fell to Mary. And she took them and returned home. Now it was at this time that Zechariah became mute, and Samuel took his place until Zechariah regained his speech. Meanwhile, Mary had taken up the scarlet and was spinning it.

∽ 11 ∾

AND SHE TOOK HER WATER JAR AND went out to fill it with water. Suddenly there was a voice saying to her, "Greetings, favored one! The Lord is with you. Blessed are you among women." Mary began looking around, both right and left, to see where the voice was coming from. She became terrified and went home. After putting the water jar down and taking up the purple thread, she sat down on her chair and began to spin.

A heavenly messenger suddenly stood before her: "Don't be afraid, Mary. You see, you've found favor in the sight of the Lord of all. You will conceive by means of his word."

But as she listened, Mary was doubtful and said, "If I actually conceive by the Lord, the living God, will I also give birth the way women usually do?"

And the messenger of the Lord replied, "No, Mary, because the power of God will overshadow you. Therefore, the child to be born will be called holy, a son of the Most High. And you will name him Jesus—the name means 'he will save his people from their sins.' "

And Mary said, "Here I am, the Lord's slave before him. I pray that all you've told me comes true."

๛ 12 ๛

AND SHE FINISHED SPINNING THE PUR-
ple and the scarlet thread and took her
work up to the high priest. The high priest
accepted them and praised her and said,
"Mary, the Lord God has extolled your name
and so you'll be blessed by all the generations
of the earth."

Mary rejoiced and left to visit her relative Elizabeth. She knocked at the door. Elizabeth heard her, tossed aside the scarlet thread,
ran to the door, and opened it for her. And
she blessed her and said, "Who am I that the
mother of my Lord should visit me? You see,

the baby inside me has jumped for joy and blessed you."

But Mary forgot the mysteries which the heavenly messenger Gabriel had spoken, and she looked up to heaven and said, "Who am I, Lord, that every generation on earth will bless me?"

She spent three months with Elizabeth. And day by day her womb kept swelling. And so Mary became frightened, returned home, and hid from the people of Israel. She was sixteen years old when these mysterious things happened to her.

∾ 13 ∾

S HE WAS IN HER SIXTH MONTH WHEN ONE day Joseph came home from his building projects, entered his house, and found her pregnant. He struck himself in the face, threw himself to the ground on sackcloth, and began to cry bitterly: "What sort of face should I present to the Lord God? What prayer can I say on her behalf since I received her as a virgin from the temple of the Lord God and didn't protect her? Who has set this trap for me? Who has done this evil deed in my house? Who has lured this virgin away from me and violated her? The story of Adam has been repeated in my case, hasn't it? For just as Adam was praying when the serpent came and found Eve alone, deceived her, and corrupted her, so the same thing has happened to me."

So Joseph got up from the sackcloth and summoned her and said to her, "God has taken a special interest in you—how could you have done this? Have you forgotten the Lord your God? Why have you brought shame on yourself, you who were raised in the Holy of Holies and fed by a heavenly messenger?"

But she began to cry bitter tears: "I am innocent. I haven't had sex with any man."

And Joseph said to her, "Then where did the child you're carrying come from?"

And she replied, "As the Lord my God lives, I don't know where it came from."

Ꙩ 14 Ꙩ

AND JOSEPH BECAME VERY FRIGHTENED and no longer spoke with her as he pondered what he was going to do with her. And Joseph said to himself, "If I try to cover up her sin, I'll end up going against the law of the Lord. But if I disclose her condition to the people of Israel, I'm afraid that the child inside her might be heaven-sent and I'll end up handing innocent blood over to a death sentence. So what should I do with her? I know, I'll divorce her quietly."

But when night came a messenger of the Lord suddenly appeared to him in a dream and said: "Don't be afraid of this girl, because the child in her is the holy spirit's doing. She will have a son and you will name him Jesus—the name means 'he will save his people from their sins.'" And Joseph got up from his sleep and praised the God of Israel who had given him this favor. And so he began to protect the girl.

∽ 15 ∾

THEN ANNAS THE SCHOLAR CAME TO him and said to him, "Joseph, why haven't you attended our assembly?"

And he replied to him, "Because I was worn out from the trip and rested my first day home."

Then Annas turned and saw that Mary was pregnant.

He left in a hurry for the high priest and said to him, "You remember Joseph, don't you—the man you yourself vouched for? Well, he's committed a serious offense."

And the high priest asked, "In what way?"

"Joseph has violated the virgin he received from the temple of the Lord," he replied. "He had his way with her and hasn't disclosed his action to the people of Israel."

And the high priest asked him, "Has Joseph really done this?"

And he replied, "Send temple assistants and you'll find the virgin pregnant."

And so the temple assistants went and found her just as Annas had reported, and then they brought her, along with Joseph, to the court.

"Mary, why have you done this?" the high priest asked her. "Why have you humiliated yourself? Have you forgotten the Lord your God, you who were raised in the Holy of the Holies and fed by heavenly messengers? You of all people, you who heard their hymns and danced for them—why have you done this?"

And she wept bitterly: "As the Lord God lives, I stand innocent before him. Believe me, I've not had sex with any man."

And the high priest said, "Joseph, why have you done this?"

And Joseph said, "As the Lord lives, I am innocent where she is concerned."

And the high priest said, "Don't perjure yourself, but tell the truth. You've had your way with her and haven't disclosed this action to the people of Israel. And you haven't humbled yourself under God's mighty hand, so that your offspring might be blessed."

But Joseph was silent.

ဆ 16 ၰ

T HEN THE HIGH PRIEST SAID, "RETURN
the virgin you received from the temple
of the Lord."

And Joseph burst into tears. . . .

And the high priest said, "I'm going to
give you the Lord's drink test, and it will disclose your sin clearly to both of you."

And the high priest took the water and
made Joseph drink it and sent him into the

wilderness, but he returned unharmed. And he made the girl drink it, too, and sent her into the wilderness. She also came back unharmed. And everybody was surprised because their sin had not been revealed. And so the high priest said, "If the Lord God has not exposed your sin, then neither do I condemn you." And he dismissed them. Joseph took Mary and returned home celebrating and praising the God of Israel.

∽ 17 ∾

NOW AN ORDER CAME FROM THE Emperor Augustus that everybody in Bethlehem of Judea be enrolled in the census. And Joseph wondered, "I'll enroll my sons, but what am I going to do with this girl? How will I enroll her? As my wife? I'm ashamed to do that. As my daughter? The people of Israel know she's not my daughter. How this matter is to be decided depends on the Lord."

And so he saddled his donkey and had her get on it. His son led it and Samuel tailed along behind. As they neared the three mile marker, Joseph turned around and saw that she was sulking. And he said to himself, "Perhaps the baby she is carrying is causing her discomfort." Joseph turned around again and saw her laughing and said to her, "Mary, what's going on with you? One minute I see you're laughing and the next minute you're sulking."

And she replied, "Joseph, it's because I imagine two peoples in front of me, one weeping and mourning and the other celebrating and jumping for joy."

Halfway through the trip Mary said to him, "Joseph, help me down from the donkey— the child inside me is about to be born."

And he helped her down and said to her, "Where will I take you to give you some privacy, since this place is out in the open?"

๛ 18 ๛

HE FOUND A CAVE NEARBY AND TOOK her inside. He stationed his sons to guard her and went to look for a Hebrew midwife in the country around Bethlehem.

"Now I, Joseph, was walking along and yet not going anywhere. I looked up at the vault of the sky and saw it standing still, and then at the clouds and saw them paused in amazement, and the birds of the sky suspended in midair. As I looked on the earth, I saw a bowl lying there and workers reclining around it with their hands in the bowl; some were chewing and yet did not chew; some were picking up something to eat and yet did not pick it up; and some were putting food in their mouths and yet did not do so. Instead, they were all looking upward.

"I saw sheep being driven along and yet the sheep stood still; the shepherd was lifting his hand to strike them, and yet his hand remained raised. Then I observed the current of the river and saw goats with their mouths in the water and yet they were not drinking. Then all of a sudden everything and everybody went on with what they had been doing."

∽ 19 ∾

"THEN I SAW A WOMAN COMING down from the hill country, and she asked, 'Where are you going, sir?'

"And I replied, 'I'm looking for a Hebrew midwife.'

"She inquired, 'Are you an Israelite?'

"I told her, 'Yes.'

"And she said, 'And who's the one having a baby in the cave?'

"I replied, 'My fiancée.'

"And she continued, 'She isn't your wife?'

"I said to her, 'She is Mary, who was raised in the temple of the Lord; I obtained her by lot as my wife. But she's not really my wife; she's pregnant by the holy spirit.'

"The midwife said, 'Really?'"

Joseph responded, "Come and see."

And the midwife went with him. As they stood in front of the cave, a dark cloud overshadowed it. The midwife said, "I've really been privileged, because today my eyes have seen a miracle in that salvation has come to Israel."

Suddenly the cloud withdrew from the cave and an intense light appeared inside the cave, so that their eyes could not bear to look. And a little later that light receded until an infant became visible; he took the breast of his mother Mary.

Then the midwife shouted: "What a great day this is for me because I've seen this new miracle!"

And the midwife left the cave and met Salome and said to her, "Salome, Salome, let me tell you about a new marvel: a virgin has given birth, and you know that's impossible!"

And Salome replied, "As the Lord my God lives, unless I insert my finger and examine her, I will never believe that a virgin has given birth."

✌ 20 ✍

THE MIDWIFE ENTERED AND SAID, "MARY, position yourself for an examination. You are facing a serious test."

And so Mary, when she heard these instructions, positioned herself, and Salome inserted her finger into Mary. And then Salome cried aloud and said, "Woe is me because of my transgression and my disbelief; I have put the living God on trial. Look! My hand is disappearing! It's being consumed by flames!"

Then Salome fell on her knees in the presence of the Lord, with these words, "God of my ancestors, remember me because I'm a descendant of Abraham, Isaac, and Jacob. Don't make an example of me for the people of Israel, but give me a place among the poor again. You yourself know, Lord, that I've been healing people in your name and have been receiving my payment from you."

And suddenly a messenger from the Lord appeared, saying to her, "Salome, Salome, the Lord of all has heard your prayer. Hold out your hand to the child and pick him up, and then you'll have salvation and joy."

Salome approached the child and picked him up with these words, "I'll worship him because he's been born to be king of Israel." And Salome was instantly healed and left the cave vindicated.

Then a voice said abruptly, "Salome, Salome, don't report the marvels you've seen until the child goes to Jerusalem."

∽ 21 ∾

JOSEPH WAS ABOUT READY TO DEPART for Judea when a great uproar was about to take place in Bethlehem in Judea. It all started when magi came inquiring, "Where is the newborn king of the Judeans? We're here because we saw his star in the East and have come to pay him homage."

When Herod heard about their visit, he was terrified and sent agents to the magi. He also sent for the high priests and questioned them in his palace: "What's been written about the Anointed? Where is he supposed to be born?"

They said to him, "In Bethlehem, Judea, that's what the scriptures say." And he dismissed them.

Then he questioned the magi: "What sign have you seen regarding the one who has been born king?"

And the magi said, "We saw a star of exceptional brilliance in the sky, and it so dimmed the other stars that they disappeared. Consequently, we know that a king was born for Israel. And we have come to pay him homage."

Herod instructed them: "Go and begin your search, and if you find him, report back to me, so that I can also go and pay him homage."

The magi departed. And there it was: the star they had seen in the East led them on until they came to the cave; then the star stopped directly above the head of the child. After the magi saw him with his mother Mary, they took gifts out of their pouches—gold, pure incense, and myrrh.

Since they had been advised by the heavenly messenger not to go into Judea, they returned to their country by another route.

ᴔ 22 ᴖ

WHEN HEROD REALIZED HE HAD BEEN duped by the astrologers, he flew into a rage and dispatched his executioners with instructions to kill all the infants two years old and younger.

When Mary heard that the infants were being killed, she was frightened and took her child, wrapped him in strips of cloth, and placed him in a feeding trough used by cattle.

As for Elizabeth, when she heard that they were looking for John, she took him and went up into the hill country. She kept searching for a place to hide him, but there was none to be had. Then she groaned and said out loud, "Mountain of God, please take in a mother with her child." You see, Elizabeth was unable to keep on climbing because her nerve failed her. But suddenly the mountain was split open and let them in. This mountain allowed the light to shine through to her, since a messenger of the Lord was with them for protection.

∽ 23 ∾

HEROD, THOUGH, KEPT LOOKING FOR John and sent his agents to Zechariah serving at the altar with this message for him: "Where have you hidden your son?"

But he answered them, "I am a minister of God, attending to his temple. How should I know where my son is?"

And so the agents left and reported all this to Herod, who became angry and said, "Is his son going to rule over Israel?"

And he sent his agents back with this message for him: "Tell me the truth. Where is your son? Don't you know that I have your life in my power?"

And the agents went and reported this message to him.

Zechariah answered, "I am a martyr for God. Take my life. The Lord, though, will receive my spirit because you are shedding innocent blood at the entrance to the temple of the Lord."

And so at daybreak Zechariah was murdered, but the people of Israel did not know that he had been murdered.

✍ 24 ✎

A T THE HOUR OF FORMAL GREETINGS
the priests departed, but Zechariah
did not meet and bless them as was custom-
ary. And so the priests waited around for
Zechariah, to greet him with prayer and to
praise the Most High God.

But when he did not show up, they all
became fearful. One of them, however, summoned up his courage, entered the sanctuary,
and saw dried blood next to the Lord's altar.
And a voice said, "Zechariah has been murdered! His blood will not be cleaned up until
his avenger appears."

When he heard this utterance he was
afraid and went out and reported to the
priests what he had seen and heard. They
also summoned up their courage, entered,

and saw what had happened. The panels of the temple cried out, and the priests ripped their robes from top to bottom. They did not find his corpse, but they did find his blood, now turned to stone. They were afraid and went out and reported to the people that Zechariah had been murdered. When all the tribes of the people heard this, they began to mourn; and they beat their breasts for three days and three nights.

After three days, however, the priests deliberated about whom they should appoint to the position of Zechariah. The lot fell to Simeon. This man, you see, is the one who was informed by the holy spirit that he would not see death until he had laid eyes on the Anointed in the flesh.

✌ 25 ✍

Now I, James, am the one who wrote this account at the time when an uproar arose in Jerusalem at the death of Herod. I took myself to the wilderness until the uproar in Jerusalem died down. There I praised the Lord God, who gave me the wisdom to write this account.

Grace will be with all those who fear the Lord. Amen.

About the Translation

T his translation is part of the Scholars Version translation, published by Polebridge Press. An original translation of all the canonical and non-canonical Gospel texts, the Scholars Version is the first major new translation of these texts prepared without ecclesiastical or religious control. The translation offers the modern reader the opportunity to experience the original vitality and spirit of these texts. The fresh and contemporary language of these translations is being used by a growing number of writers and scholars.

The Scholars Version translation of the Infancy Gospel of James appears in *The Infancy Gospel of James and Thomas*, published by Polebridge Press. As part of the Scholars Bible series, the book presents the translated Gospel side-by-side with the original language text, along with introduction, notes and glossary.

The Scholars Version translation of all the known Gospels and Gospel fragments from the early Christian era, including the Infancy Gospel of James, appears in *The Complete Gospels*, edited by Robert J. Miller and published by Polebridge Press.

For information about these books and the Scholars Version translations, contact Polebridge Press, P.O. Box 6144, Santa Rosa, CA 95406.

About the Author

R ONALD F. HOCK is professor of religion at the University of Southern California, where he teaches courses on the origins of Christianity, the world of the New Testament, and ancient Greek religion. He holds a Ph.D. from Yale University in New Testament studies and is a leading authority on the social and intellectual world of the New Testament. His most recent book is *The Infancy Gospels of James and Thomas* (Polebridge Press, 1995). He is currently writing books on the apocryphal Gospel of Peter as well as on ancient education.

OTHER ULYSSES PRESS TITLES

Jesus and Buddha: The Parallel Sayings
Marcus Borg, Editor   Introduction by Jack Kornfield

Traces the life stories and beliefs of Jesus and Buddha, then presents a comprehensive collection of their remarkably similar teachings on facing pages. *Hardcover. $19.95*

The Lost Gospel Q: The Original Sayings of Jesus
Marcus Borg, Editor   Introduction by Thomas Moore

The sayings within this book represent the very first Gospel. Here is the original Sermon on the Mount, the Lord's Prayer and Beatitudes. Reconstructed by biblical historians, Q provides a window into the world of ancient Christianity. *Hardcover. $15.00*

Four Faces: A Journey in Search of Jesus
Mark Tully   Introduction by Thomas Moore

BBC journalist Mark Tully travels the globe to bring together the most current theories about Jesus, drawing on ancient texts, modern archaeology and interviews with historians, theologians and holy men. *$15.00*

4000 Years of Christmas: A Gift From the Ages
Earl W. Count and Alice Lawson Count   Introduction by Dan Wakefield

Tracing myths and folklore from the Near East to northern Europe, this beautiful volume reveals the surprising origins of our modern Christmas holiday. *Hardcover. $16.00*

A Boy Named Jesus: How the Early Years Shaped His Life
Robert Aron   Introduction by Bishop John Shelby Spong

A distinguished historian explores the elements that would have shaped Jesus' life. He notes how a boy rooted in the Jewish tradition laid the foundation for an entirely new religion. *$14.00*

To order these or other Ulysses Press books call 800-377-2542 or write to Ulysses Press, P.O. Box 3440, Berkeley, CA 94703-3440. There is no charge for shipping on retail orders. California residents must include sales tax. Allow two to three weeks for delivery.